✳ Smithsonian

THE CIVIL RIGHTS MOVEMENT

THEN AND NOW

BY DAN ELISH

CONSULTANT:
CHRISTOPHER WILSON, DIRECTOR OF EXPERIENCE DESIGN,
NATIONAL MUSEUM OF AMERICAN HISTORY

CAPSTONE PRESS
a capstone imprint

Smithsonian is published by Capstone Press,
1710 Roe Crest Drive, North Mankato, Minnesota 56003
www.mycapstone.com

Library of Congress Cataloging-in-Publication Data
Cataloging-in-publication is on file with the Library of Congress.
ISBN 978-1-5435-0387-6 (library binding)
ISBN 978-15435-0391-3 (paperback)
ISBN 978-1-5435-0395-1 (ebook pdf)

Editorial Credits
Michelle Bisson, editor; Russell Griesmer, designer; Svetlana Zhurkin,
media researcher; Laura Manthe, production specialist

Photo Credits
Getty Images: Anadolu Agency/Samuel Corum, 48, The LIFE Images Collection/Carl
Iwasaki, 17; LBJ Library photo by Yoichi Okamoto, 33; Library of Congress, cover
(top right), 1 (bottom), 8, 27, 29, 41; Newscom: Everett Collection, 4, 14, 20, 24, 31, 38,
Icon SMI/Sporting News Archives, 16, Reuters/Gary Cameron, 51, Reuters/Pool,
34, Zuma Press/The Commercial Appeal, 19; Shutterstock: Christopher Halloran,
42, Everett Historical, 11, 13, 52, Ira Bostic, 47, Ivonne Wierink, cover (left), 1 (top),
Joseph Sohm, 57, Morphart Creation, 6
Design Elements by Capstone and Shutterstock

Printed in the United States of America.
010844S18

TABLE OF CONTENTS

The local sheriff's posse stood over an injured protester in Selma, Alabama.

CHAPTER 1

A NEED FOR CHANGE

Enough was enough.

It was 1965 and southern blacks were understandably angry. Yes, a major civil rights bill had finally passed Congress the year before, outlawing segregation in schools, restaurants, and public places. But what good were those equal rights if black Americans were still unable to exercise the most valuable freedom of all: the right to vote. True, the Civil War, fought a hundred years earlier, had brought an end to slavery. But how did that help African Americans when southern states passed a series of laws requiring blacks to pay poll taxes and pass absurd literacy tests full of trick questions as a way to keep them from going to the polls?

Something had to give—especially when, on February 26, 1965, civil rights activist Jimmie Lee Jackson was murdered in Alabama, shot by a highway patrolman during a peaceful march for equality. With tempers flaring, civil rights leaders James Bevel and Diane Nash called for a march—a long one too—to highlight the need for voting rights. The route they picked was from Selma, Alabama, to the state capital of Montgomery, 56 miles away. But on March 7 the first group of marchers was viciously attacked by police with billy clubs and tear

The history of blacks in America began with their kidnapping in Africa in the 1600s. It was a very long road to freedom and civil rights.

gas, an event so horrific it came to be called "Bloody Sunday." As *Time* magazine put it, "Rarely in human history has public opinion reacted so spontaneously and with such fury." Indeed, with outrage building, the marchers tried again on March 10.

But this time civil rights leader Martin Luther King Jr. turned the marchers back, unwilling to defy a federal court injunction blocking the march, angering student protesters and others who had traveled there to fight. Still, King waited, seeking the protection of federal troops before setting out on the dangerous journey. White supremacists, men and women who wanted the nation to remain a two-tiered, segregated society, were riled up. That night, white civil rights activist James Reeb, a minister, was beaten to death. In response, on March 15, President Lyndon B. Johnson asked Congress to pass a national voting rights bill.

He also granted the marchers the federal protection they wanted. On March 21, accompanied by 1,900 members of the National Guard, King and the group of protesters left Selma for the long trek to Montgomery. Walking down Route 80, known locally as "the Jefferson Davis Highway," the marchers arrived in Montgomery on March 24. In the end, 25,000 people arrived at the state capital to take a stand for equal voting rights. That August President Johnson signed the Voting Rights Act, a law that finally guaranteed the right to vote to every American citizen. It had

THE CIVIL RIGHTS MOVEMENT

Many historians believe that the signing of the Voting Rights Act in 1965 marked the culmination of the civil rights movement, a period after World War II in which black Americans and white supporters joined together to fight for equal rights for African Americans. Black men and women had fought bravely in World War II, but they returned from overseas to find themselves still treated as second-class citizens in their own country. In the South, African Americans were forced to attend separate schools, eat at separate restaurants, sit in the back of buses, and drink from water fountains marked "colored." King and other leaders fought for civil rights through peaceful means, slowly but surely building a consensus for change, forcing the federal government to integrate long-segregated institutions and to guarantee the right to vote to every black American.

taken "only" 100 years after slavery was abolished to become law.

A SAD HISTORY

Though the "new world" was a destination of choice for European whites, blacks did not make the trip of their own free will. Rather, they were kidnapped by African traders and shipped to the Americas to be sold into slavery. Before long the economy of the southern United States depended upon slave labor. Blacks weren't just second-class citizens—they weren't citizens at all, working the fields under the overseer's lash. Though there were early abolitionists—men and women who fought for slavery's end—many of America's Founding Fathers owned slaves themselves. And when it came time to write the U.S. Constitution in 1787, divisions between the North and

Southerners in Savannah, Georgia, raising the Confederate flag

South were so bitter that a compromise was struck: to calculate representation in Congress, black men were deemed to be worth only 3/5ths a white man. Women of any race were not counted at all.

LURCHING TOWARD CIVIL WAR

From the end of the Revolutionary War through the middle of the 1800s, tensions between the North and South grew. To keep political power between the two sections of the country equal, great effort was taken to keep the number of "slave" and "free" states the same. In 1820 Congress passed the Missouri Compromise, a law that, among other things, kept the peace by admitting Maine as a free state while allowing Missouri to have slaves. Thirty years later, with the Compromise of 1850, Congress did its

ELI WHITNEY

In colonial times it was very hard to remove the tiny seeds that grew in each individual cotton plant. An inventor named Eli Whitney came to the rescue in 1794 with his cotton gin, a machine that expertly removed seeds from cotton, thereby giving a huge boost to southern plantations. With cotton easier to produce, business boomed, requiring even more slaves to tend to the fields. It hadn't been his intention, but Whitney's invention helped prolong the institution of slavery.

best to equally divide up land acquired in the Mexican War, predominantly the modern-day southwest and California. But by 1860 tensions had risen to a breaking point. In December, shortly after Abraham Lincoln was elected president, South Carolina seceded from the Union. It was soon followed by the rest of the South. The 11 states that called themselves the Confederacy held a constitutional convention at which they elected Jefferson Davis president. Just after Lincoln assumed the presidency of the United States in March 1861, the Civil War began.

It was tough going for the North at first. Though possessed of superior manpower and a stronger industrial base, the North suffered through a series of subpar generals, notably George McClellan. He was content to have his troops march in formation in the fields around Washington, D.C., rather than engage the South in battle. Eventually, Lincoln found an excellent military leader in Ulysses S. "Unconditional Surrender" Grant. As Lincoln put it, "I can't spare this man, he fights."

In January 1863 Lincoln signed the Emancipation Proclamation, a document that gave southern slaves their freedom as well as the North a concrete cause to fight for. Finally, after much carnage and more than 600,000 dead, southern general Robert E. Lee surrendered to General Grant at Appomattox, Virginia, on April 9, 1865. The Civil War was over. On December 6, 1865, the 13th Amendment to the Constitution was ratified, abolishing slavery. In 1866 the 14th Amendment guaranteed equal rights to former slaves. In 1870 Congress ratified the 15th Amendment, which guaranteed African American men the right to vote. It seemed that the country was finally experiencing what Abraham Lincoln had called "a new birth of freedom."

RECONSTRUCTION AND JIM CROW

No one knows how history might have been different if Lincoln hadn't been killed on April 14, 1865, by John Wilkes Booth, a southern fanatic for the Confederate cause. Lincoln might have overseen the southern reentry or "reconstruction" into the Union with a gentler touch. As it was, in 1877, after years of sometimes brutal occupation, northern troops left the South. This allowed southern state governments to pass a series of laws known as Jim Crow that stripped African Americans of the rights that had been won in the Civil War. Under Jim Crow, the South became entirely segregated. Slavery was illegal, but African Americans were not allowed to go to the same schools or live in the same neighborhoods as whites. Other laws said that a black man wasn't allowed to shake hands with a white man or light a white woman's cigarette. These laws were really about white supremacy.

In 1896 the Supreme Court gave legal sanction to this shameful system of discrimination. Homer

THE KU KLUX KLAN

Under the guise of defending the southern way of life, the Ku Klux Klan was a white supremacist group that brutalized black southerners and their white sympathizers for decades. A black man accused of a crime was rarely given a fair trial. Guilty or not, black people were often lynched, chased down by Klan members, and hanged. Klan activity continued in the 1950s and 1960s as dissatisfied whites fought against the gains of the civil rights movement. America's first and foremost terrorist organization, the Ku Klux Klan, dedicated itself to subjugating others through intimidation and violence.

Plessy was arrested when he tried to sit in the "white only" section of a train in Louisiana. In time his case made it all the way to the Supreme Court. In *Plessy v. Ferguson* the Court introduced the concept of "separate

but equal," ruling that states could legally separate citizens as long as both races had access to schools, restaurants, and transportation of equal quality. Of course, in the South and parts of the North in those days, the separate accommodations enjoyed by whites were dramatically better than those endured by blacks. As the lone dissenting judge on the Supreme Court, John Harlan, wrote:

❝ The thin disguise of 'equal' accommodations ... will not mislead anyone, nor atone for the wrong this day done. ❞

Indeed, for the next 60 years, in a South ruled by Jim Crow and *Plessy v. Ferguson*, blacks were second-class citizens unable to enjoy the fruits of American democracy.

Black children were put in chain gangs and forced to labor in fields in the Jim Crow South at the turn of the 20th century.

REPUBLIC

GREATEST PICTURE OF ALL TIME "THE BIRTH OF A NATION"

The GREATEST PICTURE OF ALL TIME

"BIRTH OF A NATION" PREACHES RACE HATRED NAACP

THIS FILM INSULTS NEGRO AMERICANS

NAACP members protested the playing of the racist *Birth of A Nation* in New York City in 1947.

After *Plessy v. Ferguson* sanctioned a system of institutionalized racism in the United States, black Americans began to realize something important: their only hope of securing equal rights was to organize. In 1909 the NAACP (National Association for the Advancement of Colored People) was founded, its mission to secure blacks the rights promised by the 13th, 14th, and 15th amendments. In one of its first fights, the organization tried to get theaters to stop showing *The Birth of a Nation*, a 1915 three-hour silent movie that inaccurately presented the South as a place where the Ku Klux Klan was heroic and blacks were frightening monsters. Though unsuccessful in stopping the movie viewings—in fact, *The Birth of a Nation* was the first American blockbuster— one of the NAACP's leaders, Charles Houston, died confident of ultimate success. He wrote, "We may not win today or tomorrow but the storm gathers and all the pride and power of prejudice will be swept away." Indeed, over time the NAACP's legal efforts were instrumental in getting important civil rights legislation passed.

Slowly but surely, there were glimmers of progress. In 1947 Jackie Robinson became the first African

Jackie Robinson

Linda Brown of Topeka, Kansas, lived seven blocks from the nearest school. Even so, the young girl was forced to walk 21 blocks each day to a neighboring school that was notably inferior. The reason? Linda Brown was black and the school near her house was for whites only. In 1952 a young lawyer named Thurgood Marshall—later the first black justice on the U.S. Supreme Court—took up the case called *Brown v. Board of Education*.

American to play Major League baseball. In 1948 President Harry Truman issued executive orders banning racism in the military. But it wasn't until the 1950s, with white America enjoying a period of unparalleled prosperity, that the civil rights movement truly caught fire.

Arguing before the Supreme Court, Marshall attacked the concept of "separate but equal," making the point that separate almost always meant unequal—especially in the South. On May 17, 1954, Chief Justice Earl Warren led the court to a unanimous decision that shook the world. "In the

Linda Brown (left) posed with her family in front of their house in 1954.

field of public education the doctrine of separate but equal has no place," Warren wrote. "Separate educational facilities are inherently unequal." He was right. According to historian Kenneth C. Davis, "Schools for whites were spanking new, well maintained, properly staffed, and amply supplied. Black schools were usually single-room shacks with no toilets, only one teacher, and a broken chalkboard. If black parents wanted their children to be warm in the winter, they had to buy their own coal."

THE MURDER OF EMMETT TILL

In 1955, a 14-year-old African American boy from Chicago traveled south to Money, Mississippi, to visit relatives. A white woman, Carolyn Bryant, said Emmett Till grabbed her hand in a local grocery store. That night the woman's husband and half-brother kidnapped and murdered the boy. Though the coroner wanted to bury him in Mississippi, Emmett's mother insisted that his body be shipped back to Chicago for an open casket funeral. When a picture of the boy's brutally disfigured face was published in *Jet* magazine, an outcry against racially motivated violence swept the land. But were the murderers sent to prison? No, both men were found not guilty by a local jury. Even worse, once free they confessed to the murder to a reporter from *Look* magazine in exchange for a hefty fee.

But the story wasn't over. In 2017 Carolyn, age 82, admitted that she had lied when she told the police of the day that Emmett had grabbed her hand and spoken crudely. "That part," she said, "is not true."

"I was hoping that one day she would admit it," said Wheeler Parker, a cousin of Emmett's, now an older man. "It's important to people understanding how the word of a white person against a black person was law, and a lot of black people lost their lives because of it. It really speaks to history, it shows what black people went through in those days."

It had taken nearly 60 years, but the Supreme Court had finally overturned *Plessy v. Ferguson*. While many Americans who were in favor of integration cheered, many southern whites weren't pleased. "Human blood may stain southern soil…," the *Daily News* of Jackson, Mississippi, wrote in an editorial, "but the dark red stains of that blood will be on the marble steps on the United States Supreme Court Building." In 1956 Strom Thurmond, a Republican senator from South Carolina, issued a document he titled "A Southern Manifesto," which called on southerners to resist integration by any means. Fortunately for them, the Supreme Court had not specified a definite timetable for integration. States were called on to use "all deliberate speed" to integrate their schools and public buildings. For many in the South, "all deliberate speed" meant never.

Carolyn Bryant sat next to her husband, accused murderer Roy Bryant, who holds their children, during court proceedings.

THE MONTGOMERY BUS BOYCOTT

From the days of World War II through the mid-1950s, African Americans in Montgomery, Alabama, protested segregated bus lines. In early 1955 a 15-year-old named Claudette Colvin told a driver who asked her to change seats, "I done paid my dime, I ain't got no reason to move." When Colvin was arrested, local African American lawyers considered taking her case to federal court to prove that segregated buses were illegal under the U.S. Constitution. But then it was discovered that Colvin was pregnant. Worried that the white press would portray her as a "bad girl," lawyers decided to wait to present their case.

Rosa Parks was a well-educated woman of 43 who had worked for years as a secretary at the local chapter of the Montgomery NAACP. On December 1, 1955, it was Parks'

Members of the First Baptist Church of Montgomery, Alabama, gave a standing ovation to the leaders of the bus boycott.

turn to refuse to give up her seat on a public bus to a white man, saying that "she was tired of giving in." She later recalled:

"When he [the bus driver] saw me still sitting, he asked if I was going to stand up, and I said, 'No, I'm not.' And he said, 'Well, if you don't stand up, I'm going to have to call the police and have you arrested.' I said, 'You may do that.'"

Parks' refusal changed history. News of her arrest soon reached E.D. Nixon, who had been the head of the NAACP when Parks was secretary. After bailing her out of jail, Nixon said to Parks, "With your permission we can break down segregation on the bus with your case." And so it began. That night an African American woman named Jo Ann Robinson called the leaders of the Women's Political Council. Together they decided to stage a boycott of the Montgomery bus lines, starting that coming Monday.

Robinson stayed up all night, using a mimeograph to copy 35,000 handbills that urged African Americans to stay off the public buses. Robinson's flier read, in part:

"This is for Monday, Dec. 5, 1955. Another Negro woman has been arrested and thrown into jail because she refused to get up out of her seat for a white person to sit down. It is the second time since the Claudette Colvin case that a Negro woman has been arrested for the same thing. This has to be stopped.

"…We are therefore asking every Negro to stay off the buses Monday in protest of the arrest and trial. Don't ride the buses to work, to town, to school, or anywhere on Monday…"

It was a bold plan. That Monday virtually none of the 50,000 black

BAYARD RUSTIN

Bayard Rustin is one of the lesser-known heroes of the civil rights era. Born on March 17, 1912, in West Chester, Pennsylvania, Rustin moved to New York City in the 1930s and quickly got active in peaceful protests for equality. An early believer in the nonviolent philosophy espoused by Indian independence leader Mahatma Gandhi, Rustin fought against racial discrimination in war-related hiring in World War II and was punished for failing to register for the draft. By 1947 he protested segregated southern transit systems and was sentenced to work on a chain gang for his efforts. Then in 1953 Rustin was arrested again, this time for living as an openly gay man. But he never gave up fighting for his progressive beliefs. In 1958 Rustin coordinated a march in Aldermaston, England, protesting nuclear weapons. Throughout the 1950s and 1960s, Rustin served as one of Martin Luther King Jr.'s most important advisers. Rustin died in 1987.

citizens of Montgomery rode the public buses, depriving the city of their fares. Before long, the one-day boycott had stretched to weeks and then months. With the bus company refusing to integrate or even hire black drivers to service routes through African American neighborhoods, black riders stayed away in droves, finding other ways to get around town: carpools, taxis, and walking.

The boycott brought a new and exciting leader to the fore. Twenty-six-year-old Martin Luther King Jr. was a new minister in town, but already known as a brilliant public speaker. To help support the boycott, a new organization, the Montgomery Improvement Association, was formed and King was named its leader. King quickly realized how the nonviolent tactics used by Indian nationalist Mahatma Gandhi could

be used by southern blacks. King rallied the forces with stirring speeches that laid out the issue in stark moral terms.

66 The only weapon that we have in our hands this evening is the weapon of protest," King said. "We are not wrong. . .in what we are doing. If we are wrong the Supreme Court of this nation is wrong. If we are wrong the Constitution of the United States is wrong. If we are wrong, God Almighty is wrong! 99

In the end, the bus boycott lasted 381 days. After losing 65 percent of its profits for more than a year, the city of Montgomery finally gave in and agreed that black riders would no longer have to sit in the back of the bus. It was a stunning success, a testament to Parks, Colvin, Nixon, Robinson, King, and many others working together, fighting for equality.

THE LITTLE ROCK NINE

In 1957 nine black students wanted to attend Central High School in Little Rock, Arkansas. Yes, the Supreme Court had ruled in *Brown v. Board of Education* that schools could not be segregated. But that didn't stop Arkansas Governor Orval Faubus from calling in the state National Guard to stop the students from enrolling. Whites protested, sometimes violently, outside the schools. Some black reporters were attacked. The president of the Arkansas branch of the NAACP, Daisy Bates, was at home the night before school was to start when a rock smashed through her window.

" I was covered with shattered glass...," Bates said. "I reached for the rock lying in the middle of the floor. A note was tied to it. . ..Scrawled in bold print were the words: 'Stone this time. Dynamite next.'"

In the face of such violence, President Dwight D. Eisenhower, who had been criticized by many for moving too slowly to support civil rights, was forced to act. In September 1957 he called in the federal National Guard. In the end, the Little Rock Nine were finally admitted to school, but only under the protection of the 101th Airborne Division of the U.S. Army.

Picketers in front of a Woolworth's in New York protested the store's segregation policies in the South.

Despite the success of the Montgomery bus boycott and President Eisenhower's use of troops to integrate the public high schools of Little Rock, the civil rights movement had a long way to go. By the end of the 1950s only 2 percent of black students in the south went to integrated schools. Segregation continued as before with blacks unable to go to the same restaurants, live in the same neighborhoods, or even use the same public bathrooms as whites. In fact, the situation in the South was so bad that Premier Nikita Khrushchev of the Soviet Union pointed to discrimination as a prime example of the many failings of democracy. After all, he argued, what was so great about a system of government that wouldn't allow certain students to attend the school that is closest?

As the 1960s began, civil rights leaders knew that they had to keep the pressure on.

THE SIT-INS AND FREEDOM RIDERS

Diane Nash was a young African American woman from Chicago. In 1959 when Nash transferred to Fisk University in Nashville, Tennessee, she was appalled by the segregation she found. In response, she began to attend workshops in nonviolent protests that were run by divinity student and civil rights activist James Lawson. From day one, Nash and the other students prepared themselves for battle. "I remember we used to role play," Nash said. "We would do things like pretend we were sitting at lunch counters, in order to prepare ourselves to do that. We would practice things such as how to protect your head from a beating." Soon Nash and other African American students began "testing the lunch counters," going into department store restaurants to attempt to be served. They never were.

At the same time, four black freshmen at the North Carolina Agricultural and Technical College, Joseph McNeil, Franklin McCain, David Richmond, and Ezell Blair Jr., had a similar idea. On February 1, 1960, they walked into an F.W. Woolworth's, bought and paid for a few small items, then sat down at the "white only" lunch counter and ordered coffee. They were refused.

"I beg your pardon," Franklin McCain said to the waitress. "You just served me at a counter two feet away [to purchase a tube of toothpaste and some school supplies]. Why is it that you serve me at one counter and deny me at another?"

There was no good answer but that didn't matter. McNeil, McCain, Richmond, and Blair were still denied service. At that time Ella Baker was the executive director of the Southern Christian Leadership Conference. Right away she began making calls to college campuses throughout the South. "What are you going to do?" she cried. "It is time to move!"

By that time Nash was head of a group called Nashville Student Movement. "When the students in Greensboro sat in on February 1st," Nash recalled, "we simply made plans to join their effort by sitting in at the same chains."

Soon a giant wave of peaceful "sit-ins" at white-only restaurants swept the South. For the next year, courageous black protesters, many of them members of an organization called the Student Nonviolent Coordinating Committee (SNCC, which is pronounced "Snick") endured streams of racist taunts and quietly demanded to be served. Joined by groups of white sympathizers, slowly

Freedom Riders barely made it to safety after their bus was firebombed by segregationists.

but surely, everyone's hard work paid off. Stores began to change their policies, agreeing to serve anyone, regardless of race. As Nash put it:

"It was a people's movement. The media and history seem to record it as Martin Luther King's movement, but young people should realize that it was people just like them, their age, that formulated goals and strategies, and actually developed the movement. When they look around now, and see things that need to be changed, they should say: 'What can I do? What can my roommate and I do to effect that change?'"

THE FREEDOM RIDERS

In 1960 the Supreme Court ruled that segregation in public bus lines violated the Equal Protection Clause of the U.S. Constitution. In the summer of 1961, the Congress of Racial Equality (CORE) initiated a series of protests to make southern bus lines and bus stations live up to the law. The plan was simple: white and black protesters called Freedom Riders would take buses into the Deep South, then get off and sit down in white-only bus waiting rooms. Simple enough but also dangerous.

As James Farmer, the founder of CORE, put it, "I think all of us were prepared for as much violence as could be thrown at us. We were prepared for the possibility of death." Indeed, on May 4, 1961, two busloads of Freedom Riders left from Washington, D.C. For the first 10 days, their trip was peaceful enough. But when they reached Anniston, Alabama, on May 14, one of the buses was firebombed. The riders barely escaped with their lives.

By this point, America had a new president, young John F. Kennedy, a Democrat. When the replacement bus reached Birmingham, Alabama, the riders were attacked by mobs with baseball bats, chains, and iron pipes. With another mob awaiting the Freedom Riders in Montgomery, Alabama, President Kennedy called in federal marshals to protect the riders. Ultimately, the riders had to take an airplane to New Orleans to finish their journey. Over the coming months, SNCC continued the Freedom Rides, achieving something significant: their journeys received enormous national exposure. As images of angry southern mobs flashed on TV screens across the country, the drumbeat for real civil rights legislation grew by the day. On May 29, 1961, the federal government called for the Interstate Commerce Commission to end segregation on buses crossing state lines.

JAMES MEREDITH

In 1962 Air Force veteran James Meredith decided to apply to the University of Mississippi. When it was discovered that he was black, Governor Ross Barnett refused to admit him, stating, "No school will be integrated in Mississippi while I am your governor." President Kennedy was forced to arrange federal protection for Meredith. Showing great personal courage, on October 1, 1962, Meredith became the first African American to enroll in the University of Mississippi.

James Meredith

"LETTER FROM A BIRMINGHAM JAIL"

While jailed in Birmingham, King wrote a famous manifesto defending his strategy on nonviolent resistance in the fight for civil rights. Called appropriately "Letter from a Birmingham Jail," King wrote:

"I am in Birmingham because injustice is here.... Birmingham is probably the most thoroughly segregated city in the United States. Its ugly record of brutality is widely known. Negroes have experienced grossly unjust treatment in the courts. There have been more unsolved bombings of Negro homes and churches in Birmingham than in any other city in the nation. These are the hard, brutal facts of the case.... Nonviolent direct action seeks to...dramatize the issue [so] that it can no longer be ignored."

EVENTS MOVE QUICKLY

With each act of peaceful protest by civil rights activists—and the violence with which they were greeted—pressure was brought to bear on Kennedy to introduce legislation that would guarantee southerners their civil rights. In April 1963 King led a peaceful protest in Birmingham, Alabama. As predicted, segregationist Public Safety Commissioner Bull Connor did not support the protesters. He looked the other way as a mob attacked and King was jailed. On May 2 a group of African American students walked from a church singing "We Shall Overcome." Connor called in the fire department. Innocent protesters were pelted with water from fire hoses and attacked by police dogs. *The New York Times* called these actions "a national disgrace."

On June 11 President Kennedy made a major civil rights speech to the American people and Congress, saying "race has no place in American life or law." He asked Congress to pass legislation that gave "all Americans the right to be served in facilities which are open to the public."

Hoping to give Kennedy another push, A. Philip Randolph, King, Bayard Rustin, and a young civil rights activist

A police officer grabbed Martin Luther King Jr. by his waistband and arrested him for leading a civil rights march.

who is now a U.S. congressman, John Lewis, called for a large-scale protest in Washington, D.C. Their goals were the passage of meaningful civil rights legislation, the elimination of school segregation, a public works program and job training for the unemployed, and a $2 an hour nationwide minimum wage. On August 28, 1963, more than a quarter of a million peaceful protesters flocked to the March on Washington.

Standing before the Lincoln Memorial, King delivered what became one of the most famous speeches in American history. "I have a dream," he thundered, "that one day this nation will rise up and live out the true meaning of its creed: 'We hold these truths to be self-evident, that all men are created equal.'… I have a dream that my four little children will one day live in a nation where they will not be judged by the color of their skin but by the content of their character. I have a dream today!"

Only three months later, on November 22, 1963, Kennedy was assassinated in Dallas, Texas. Kennedy had recently become an ally in the fight for equality. Many civil rights leaders had hoped that Kennedy would win a second term in the White House and then push hard for legislation. Worse, the new president, Lyndon Baines Johnson, was a southerner. As majority leader of the Senate in the 1950s, his record on civil rights was mixed at best. Could such a man defy his region and support serious legislation?

The answer was yes. Many historians count Johnson as one of the greatest legislators in American history, an expert at the nitty-gritty negotiating that goes into getting laws passed. On November 27, 1963, Johnson told Congress, "No memorial oration or eulogy could more eloquently honor President Kennedy's memory than the earliest possible passage of the civil rights bill for which he fought so long." With King and other civil rights leaders on his back, Johnson got to work, using Kennedy's death to push hesitant southern senators and representatives to support the new law. "This bill is going to pass if it takes us all summer …," Johnson said, "because justice and morality demand it."

On July 2 Johnson signed the Civil Rights Act of 1964, a landmark law that finally gave real legislative teeth to *Brown v. Board of Education*, outlawing discrimination based on race, color, religion, sex, or national origin.

President Lyndon B. Johnson shook Martin Luther King Jr.'s hand after signing the Civil Rights Act.

After three civil rights workers were
murdered, the killers burned their
station wagon.

CHAPTER 4

THE END OF AN ERA— SUCCESSES AND SETBACKS

The Civil Rights Act of 1964 was an unquestioned triumph. More successes followed throughout the decade. But there were also more than a few disappointments as the Vietnam War heated up overseas and the civil rights movement turned more violent back home.

THE SUMMER OF 1964

Despite success integrating schools and lunch counters, many southern states still restricted the ability of African Americans to vote. They did so by imposing poll taxes and intentionally difficult literacy tests. Many civil rights activists and concerned citizens felt strongly that the next step in the fight

for equal rights was to register black voters. After all, how could a community hope to initiate real change if an overwhelming percentage of the black residents were stopped from speaking their minds at the ballot box? On the heels of the Civil Rights Act, hundreds of young Americans, black and white, flooded the South to push for equal access to the polls. But tragedy struck—a triple murder that highlighted how unwilling many southern towns were to change the ways of Jim Crow.

It happened in June of 1964. Three young civil rights workers, Andrew Goodman and Michael Schwerner, two whites from the North, and James Chaney, a southern African American, traveled to Philadelphia, Mississippi, to register black voters. On June 21st they were picked up by police for no apparent reason, held in prison, and released. Then they disappeared. Local authorities denied accusations that they had come to harm. After all, a sheriff told President Johnson, there wasn't even a local chapter of the Ku Klux Klan in the area where the young men had disappeared. But two months later the case was broken open when Klan informers were offered $30,000 in exchange for information. Soon enough, the bodies were recovered at a nearby dam site. Despite ample evidence against 18 Klansmen, one of whom was the police chief, the state of Mississippi refused to press charges. Finally, the federal government brought civil rights charges and seven of the men were given short jail terms. Otherwise, the mob that killed Chaney, Schwerner, and Goodman escaped punishment. Decades later the state reopened the case and prosecuted one man, Edgar Ray Killen, for murder. Convicted of manslaughter, he was sentenced to 60 years in prison.

The tragedy of Chaney, Schwerner, and Goodman served as yet another wake-up call to the rest of the nation, helping push the civil rights bill to passage. But the fight wasn't over: southern blacks required the right to vote. In the spring of 1965, King decided to build momentum by leading his march from Selma to Montgomery to register black voters. Finally, on August 9, 1965, Johnson signed the Voting Rights Act, a landmark law that eliminated literacy tests and poll taxes and gave the federal government the right to oversee elections in certain counties with histories of racial bias.

PROBLEMS IN THE CITIES

After World War II many southern blacks flocked to northern cities to escape the oppression of lingering Jim Crow. Though some southern African Americans were able to find better housing and jobs—not to mention fairer treatment—others grew increasingly frustrated with the slow pace of the peaceful civil rights movement. Yes, laws had been passed.

VOTING RIGHTS LEGISLATION

On March 15, 1965, President Johnson addressed the country about the pressing need to pass meaningful voting rights legislation.

"I speak tonight for the dignity of man and the destiny of democracy.

"I urge every member of both parties— Americans of all religions and of all colors— from every section of this country—to join me in that cause.

"At times history and fate meet at a single time in a single place to shape a turning point in man's unending search for freedom. So it was at Lexington and Concord. So it was a century ago at Appomattox. So it was last week in Selma, Alabama.

"There is no Negro problem. There is no southern problem. There is no northern problem. There is only an American problem."

But had day-to-day life for black Americans really improved? For many who lived in northern ghettos, the answer was no.

In the wake of growing frustration, some blacks turned away from King to new leaders. While in prison, activist Malcolm X (born Malcolm Little in

Omaha, Nebraska) had studied the teachings of Elijah Muhammad and concluded that whites and blacks should live separately. As for peaceful protest, Malcolm X felt that blacks should be able to protect themselves "by any means necessary."

In 1965 a black activist named Stokely Carmichael ran for office in Alabama espousing "black power." As Carmichael said,

❝ I'm not going to beg the white man for anything I deserve. I'm going to take it. ❞

Stokely Carmichael spoke to a crowd at the University of California at Berkeley.

A year later, in 1966, two activists, Huey Newton and Bobby Seale, organized the Black Panther Party. Inspired by Latin American revolutionaries, Black Panthers worked behind the scenes to educate residents of poor communities about their legal rights. But they were also not afraid to carry guns to defend their communities.

As frustrations grew, rioters took to the streets. On August 11, 1965, a black motorist was stopped under suspicion of drunk driving in the Watts section of Los Angeles. A minor argument between the motorist and the police quickly escalated into a brawl. In the end it took the National Guard six days to restore peace, but not before 34 people had died and rioters had caused more than $40 million in damage. Two summers later, in 1967, riots exploded in Newark, Detroit, Chicago, New York, and Illinois.

In the wake of growing violence, King redoubled his efforts to make peaceful progress. But on April 4, 1968, he was assassinated in Memphis, Tennessee. It was a punch in the gut to the nation. Then the late president's brother, Robert Kennedy, who was running for president himself, was assassinated on June 6. The two deaths marked a grim conclusion to the robust era of civil rights. In the 1968 election between Democratic candidate Vice President Hubert Humphrey and Republican candidate Richard Nixon, the country's focus turned to Vietnam. Young Americans had been taking to the streets to protest a war they found unjust for some time. In 1968 the movement caught national attention.

BRIGHT SPOTS

Despite riots and the assassination of King, the civil rights movement did register some significant wins toward the end of the 1960s. Perhaps most important was Medicaid, a program signed into law by President Johnson in 1965 that helped poorer Americans, both black and white, with health costs. On July 30, 1965, Medicare was signed into law, providing health insurance to older Americans. In 1968 Johnson signed the Fair Housing Act, a law that sought to ensure equal access to housing for African Americans. That same year Thurgood Marshall, the lawyer who had successfully argued *Brown v. Board of Education*, became the first African American to serve on the Supreme Court.

Supreme Court Justice Thurgood Marshall

President Barack Obama

Have conditions for African Americans improved since the civil rights era? The answer is a qualified yes: conditions have improved, but there is still much work to be done. Blacks today still face discrimination by the country's police. Though not segregated, mostly black public schools are often worse than ones that are predominately white. African American men are imprisoned at a five times greater rate than whites. The most recent government statistics estimate that 745,000 African American males were behind bars in 2013.

On the other hand, the successes of the civil rights era are not to be taken for granted. Schools, restaurants, and bus lines are now integrated. No black person has to drink out of a water fountain marked "colored." Jim Crow is largely dead.

And a stunning event took place in November 2008—something that no one from the 1960s would have predicted: a black man was elected president of the United States.

BARACK OBAMA

In 2004 an obscure state senator from Illinois named Barack Hussein Obama addressed the Democratic National Convention. "Tonight is a particular honor for me," he began, "because, let's face it, my presence on this stage is pretty unlikely. My father was a foreign student, born and raised in a small village in Kenya. He grew up herding goats, went to school in a tin-roof shack. His father, my grandfather, was a cook, a domestic servant to the British." Then Obama addressed the ever-present lure of the American dream in a way that spoke to many:

"But my grandfather had larger dreams for his son. Through hard work and perseverance my father got a scholarship to study in a magical place, America, that's shown as a beacon of freedom and opportunity to so many who had come before him."

Obama's speech made him an instant star in the Democratic Party, an intelligent leader who was progressive but not extreme. After a couple of years serving as the U.S. senator from Illinois, Obama decided the time was right to run for president. With superior organization, Obama narrowly defeated Senator Hillary Clinton for the Democratic nomination. Vowing to work with Republicans to solve the nation's problems, Obama attracted voters with an upbeat slogan, "Yes We Can!" With the Republican Party suffering a backlash from a misguided war in Iraq, begun in 2003, and an economic crisis, Obama defeated Senator John McCain of Arizona. A black man was president of the United States.

As with any president, Obama had his critics. Some felt he was weak on foreign policy, too fast to withdraw troops from Iraq, and too slow to take on the terrorist group known as ISIS. But most historians agree that Obama's tenure in the White House was successful. Taking over in the midst of a financial crisis, Obama got Congress to pass a stimulus program that created jobs. He then successfully used federal funds to bail out the nation's failing auto industry.

On March 23, 2010, he signed ithe Affordable Care Act into law. This law mandated the purchase of health insurance, giving subsidies to those who could not afford market rates and imposing penalties on those who did not buy it. In 2015 Obama helped negotiate the Paris Climate Accord, the first international agreement to try to limit the gases that cause global warming.

An America in which a black man could be elected president was an America that had changed since the 1960s. Still, there was plenty of evidence throughout his presidency that bigotry was still alive and well

THE CONFEDERATE FLAG

Despite gains in the civil rights movement, monuments to the Civil War and the Confederacy still dominate many southern cities. Some white southerners argue that monuments to Confederate War heroes are important ways to honor their heritage. But many people, both whites and blacks, feel strongly that the Confederate flag—a symbol of a government that had fought to keep black Americans in bondage—is wholly inappropriate. When South Carolina governor Nikki Haley gave the order to retire the Confederate flag from the state grounds, most Americans breathed a sigh of relief. President Obama tweeted: "South Carolina taking down the confederate flag—a signal of good will and healing, and a meaningful step toward a better future."

In May 2017 New Orleans Mayor Mitch Landrieu ordered the removal of Confederate monuments in his city, saying, "The Confederacy lost and we're better for it." But there is still work to do. A demonstration turned violent on August 16, 2017, when white supremacists traveled to Charlottesville, Virginia, to protest the city's decision to take down a statue of Confederate General Robert E. Lee.

in the 21st century. Some of Obama's detractors were motivated not only by policy differences but by racial bias. Put plainly, some Americans didn't like having a black man in the White House.

TROUBLE IN BLACK NEIGHBORHOODS

The country had a black president. But many wonder if Obama's presence in the White House do much to help poor black communities. His second term was marked by a never-ending series of news reports, often caught on video, of white men or police officers murdering black civilians without cause.

Perhaps the most well-known incident occurred on the night of February 26, 2012, when a young black man named Trayvon Martin was walking unarmed through a gated community in Florida. The man on neighborhood watch that night was George Zimmerman. Falsely suspecting Martin of planning a robbery, Zimmerman shot and killed him. Outrage shook the country. How could an armed guard gun down a defenseless teen? Zimmerman pleaded self-defense, claiming that he felt Martin intended to do him harm. With no definitive proof or witnesses, Zimmerman was found not guilty by a jury and set free.

Trayvon Martin's murder was only the first of many incidents where white vigilantes or police killed a black man. On July 17, 2014, in Staten Island, New York, Eric Garner was selling loose cigarettes on the street, a crime that was usually ignored. That day, police officer Daniel Pantaleo put Garner in a chokehold that lasted about 20 seconds. Despite Garner's gurgling, "I can't breathe, I can't breathe," 11 times, Pantaleo did not release the hold in time.

When Garner died, the public outcry was enormous. Crowds marched in the streets, chanting, "I Can't Breathe." On December 3, when all charges of Pantaleo were dismissed, protests against the verdict swept the country.

RENEWED FIGHT FOR VOTING RIGHTS

Did the fight for the right of everyone to vote end when President Johnson signed the Voting Rights Act in

Marchers protested the murder of Trayvon Martin.

Thousands gathered for a candlelight vigil the week after a white supremacist march in Charlottesville, Virginia, in August 2017, resulted in the death of peaceful protester Heather Heyer.

1965? It seems not. Recently some states have passed laws that require a citizen to show a driver's license or other state ID when voting. Advocates of these tougher voting laws claim they are necessary to restrict voter fraud.

In truth, cases of voter fraud are very low. More problematic, many poorer people or people who live in urban areas don't have a driver's license. So when examined carefully, the efforts to make it harder to vote have more to do with a wish to suppress poor voters and people of color (who usually vote Democratic) than in trying to reform the system. The courts have overwhelmingly agreed, ruling in case after case against individual states' attempts to make it harder to vote.

The Supreme Court also weighed in on the issue. In a controversial 5-4 decision in 2013, the Court struck down a key component of the Voting Rights Act of 1965. Sections of the law had allowed the federal government to oversee elections in counties with a history of racial bias. But the conservative wing of the Court felt that it was time to move on. "Our country has changed," wrote Chief Justice John Roberts. "While any racial discrimination in voting is too much, Congress must ensure that the legislation it passes to remedy that problem speaks to current conditions."

In other words, Roberts argued, the era of voting discrimination was effectively over. Referring to the Voting Rights Act of 1965, Roberts agreed that the country had needed "strong medicine" to right decades of injustice. After all, when first enacted, black voter registration stood at 6.7 percent in Mississippi. But current methods of fighting racial bias had to be based on current statistics, Roberts argued. In 2013, 76 percent of African American voters were registered in Mississippi. Therefore, it was unconstitutional to require certain counties to be subjected to federal oversight at the polls.

But in a strongly worded dissent, Justice Ruth Bader Ginsberg noted that Congress had the right to decide whether a law was still necessary.

Ginsberg pointed out that in 2006 President George W. Bush signed a new Voting Rights Act, saying it was "an example of our continued commitment to a united America where every person is valued and treated with dignity and respect."

Ginsburg wrote, "Beyond question, the Voting Rights Act is no ordinary legislation. It is extraordinary because Congress embarked on a mission long delayed and of extraordinary importance: to realize the purpose and promise of the Fifteenth Amendment. … For a half century a concerted effort has been made to end racial discrimination in voting. Thanks to the Voting Rights Act, progress once the subject of a dream has been achieved and continues to be made."

BLACK LIVES MATTER

In the wake of the tragic killing of Trayvon Martin and George Zimmerman's acquittal, users of social media began using a new hashtag: #BlackLivesMatter. Very quickly, the hashtag grew into an international movement, a way of protesting police killings of African Americans and the systemic racism that often allowed it to happen. Following the 2014 deaths of Michael Brown, a black man in Ferguson, Missouri, and Eric Garner in New York City, the movement became even more well known. While many Americans embraced the spirit of Black Lives Matter, seeing with new eyes the discrimination blacks in inner cities still endure, some felt the police were being villainized. Yes, they felt, there are some bad or untrained officers out there but weren't the overwhelming majority good? As with most issues, the truth lies somewhere in between. Certainly, there are many good police officers on the streets of the U.S. On the other hand, black citizens still suffer from discrimination that, in the worst scenarios, ends in the loss of life when stopped for speeding or other minor traffic violations.

Activists for voting rights protested in front of the U.S. Supreme Court.

President Abraham Lincoln's Gettysburg Address was one of the most important speeches in U.S. history.

CHAPTER 6
WHAT'S NEXT?

In November 1863 Abraham Lincoln began the Gettysburg Address with the words, "Four score and seven years ago, our fathers brought forth a new nation, conceived in liberty and dedicated to the proposition that all men are created equal."

One could say that civil rights groups have been working ever since to ensure that the United States lives up to Lincoln's famous words, to turn the country into a place where all men and women have absolute equal rights. Great progress has been made, but the work continues as the U.S. strives toward becoming what Thomas Jefferson called "a more perfect union."

LOOKING FORWARD

As with any democracy, the power of the U.S. comes from its people. Who will show up to vote? Who fights hardest for what they want? Who will run for office? Americans are living through turbulent times. President Donald Trump won the election of 2016 in part by appealing to working-class white voters who felt that they had been ignored by both parties. But another part of President Trump's appeal was his tough—some would say discriminatory—stance on immigration. Trump's campaign promises to build a wall across the Mexican border and to institute travel

THE ACLU

The American Civil Liberties Union (ACLU) was founded in 1920, its stated mission "to defend and preserve the individual rights and liberties guaranteed to every person in this country by the Constitution and laws of the United States." Today, with more than one million members and an annual budget of over $100 million, the ACLU is active in all 50 states, the District of Columbia, and Puerto Rico. Working mostly through litigation (bringing cases to court) and lobbying (pushing members of Congress to vote in a certain way), the ACLU has become a critically important organization in the defense of basic liberties of everyday Americans.

bans against certain Muslim-majority countries have been cheered by some Americans, but condemned as racist by many more.

Even so, in terms of civil rights, there is much to feel good about. Today blacks hold more political offices than ever before. Indeed President Obama has inspired a new group of leaders to realize that achieving political power is possible for people of any race. Two of the key presidential candidates in 2016 of the Republican Party, Ted Cruz and Marco Rubio, were Hispanic. That was the first time major candidates were not white. Another major candidate, Ben Carson, was African American and drew support from whites.

Over the past few decades, the country has also made great strides in the arena of LGBTQ rights. As recently as 1999, until Vermont became the first, no state in the country allowed gay couples to even enter into a civil union, a legal agreement like marriage. On June 26, 2015—16 years later—the U.S. Supreme Court declared gay marriage itself legal.

> **Writing for a 5-4 majority, Justice Anthony M. Kennedy said, "No longer may this liberty be denied. ... No union is more profound than marriage, for it embodies the highest ideals of love, fidelity, devotion, sacrifice and family."**

It was a stunning decision, unthinkable 10 or even five years earlier.

Today women are slowly beginning to earn equal pay to men. Transgender people are beginning to be treated more fairly. And black Americans continue to fight for the same rights as white people. The fight is never easy. But all Americans can take inspiration from the civil rights era, a time when warriors of all races put their lives on the line to fight for what was right.

Because of the Civil Rights movement, new doors of opportunity and education swung open for everybody. ... Not just for blacks and whites, but also women and Latinos; and Asians and Native Americans; and gay Americans and Americans with disabilities. They swung open for you, and they swung open for me. And that's why I'm standing here today—because of those efforts, because of that legacy.

President Barack Obama

When you see something that is not right, not fair, not just, you have a moral obligation to do something about it.

Congressman John Lewis,
early leader of the civil rights movement

This nation was founded by men of many nations and backgrounds. It was founded on the principle that all men are created equal, and that the rights of every man are diminished when the rights of one man are threatened. ... It ought to be possible, in short, for every American to enjoy the privileges of being American without regard to his race or his color."

President John F. Kennedy

We all should know that diversity makes for a rich tapestry, and we must understand that all the threads of the tapestry are equal in value no matter what their color.

Maya Angelou,
African American author

Here are the values that I stand for: honesty, equality, kindness, compassion, treating people the way you want to be treated and helping those in need. To me, those are traditional values.

Ellen DeGeneres,
comedian and talk show host

At some point in our lifetime, gay marriage won't be an issue, and everyone who stood against this civil right will look as outdated as George Wallace standing on the school steps keeping James Hood from entering the Univesity of Alabama because he was black.

George Clooney, actor

I speak not for myself but for those without voice … those who have fought for their rights … their right to live in peace, their right to be treated with dignity, their right to equality of opportunity, their right to be educated.

Malala Yousafzai, Pakistani activist

Black Lives Matter and other signs were on display at a march honoring Martin Luther King Jr.

TIMELINE

1865-1870—The 13th, 14th, and 15th amendments to the U.S. Constitution are passed, ending slavery, making African Americans equal citizens, and guaranteeing black men the right to vote

1896—In *Plessy v. Ferguson*, the Supreme Court coins the concept of "separate but equal," legalizing segregation for the next 60 years

1948—President Truman calls for integration of the U.S. military

1954—In *Brown v. Board of Education*, Chief Justice Earl Warren writes the opinion for the unanimous decision striking down the concept of "separate but equal." Separate is deemed inherently unequal

1955—Rosa Parks refuses to give up her seat to a white man on a bus in Montgomery, Alabama, leading to a 381-day bus boycott. Martin Luther King Jr. emerges as the country's primary leader of the civil rights movement, calling for "peaceful resistance"

1956—The U.S. Supreme Court rules segregation on city buses unconstitutional

1957—The Little Rock Nine attend Central High School, escorted by federal troops

1960—Four students hold a sit-in at a Woolworth's in Greensboro, North Carolina

1960—John F. Kennedy is elected president, vowing to work for civil rights

1961—The Freedom Riders travel in buses to the Deep South in an attempt to integrate bus lines

April and May 1963—Martin Luther King Jr. leads a series of marches in Birmingham in which the marchers were viciously attacked by police

June 1963—President Kennedy calls for a sweeping civil rights bill

August 1963—At the March on Washington, Martin Luther King Jr. makes his "I Have a Dream" speech

November 22, 1963—President Kennedy is assassinated in Dallas

1964—President Lyndon Johnson signs the Civil Rights Bill of 1964 into law

1964—Three civil rights workers, James Chaney, Michael Schwerner, and Andrew Goodman, are murdered by the Ku Klux Klan in Mississippi

1965—Protesters march from Selma to Montgomery for the right to vote

1965—The Voting Rights Act is signed into law, guaranteeing all citizens the right to vote

1965—The first of many riots rages in Watts, Los Angeles, for six days

1967—Riots rage across the United States

1968—Martin Luther King Jr. and Robert Kennedy are assassinated

May 1992—Los Angeles riots when African American Rodney King is filmed being beaten by white police

2013—In *Shelby County v. Holder* the Supreme Court strikes down part of the 1965 Voting Rights Act

2014—The National Center for Civil and Human Rights Museum opens in Atlanta

2014—The Justice Department investigates police practices in Ferguson, Missouri, after Michael Brown, an unarmed teenager, is shot and killed

2015—The Department of Justice finds a history of discrimination in the Ferguson, Missouri, police department. Ferguson officials reach a deal with the Justice Department, avoiding a lawsuit

2016—National Museum of African American History and Culture opens as part of the Smithsonian complex of museums in Washington, D.C.

GLOSSARY

activist—a vigorous advocate of a cause, especially a political cause

boycott—to abstain from buying something or using something to achieve a certain result

compromise—settlement in which each side gives up part of its demands and agrees to the solution

consensus—general agreement

discriminate—treat a person or group unfairly, often because of race, religion, gender, sexual preference, or age

dissent—to disagree with the opinion of others

inherently—existing within something or someone as a permanent element

integrate—bring together different groups into a unified whole

manifesto—a public declaration of policy and aims, especially one issued before an election by a political party or candidate

prosperous—the state of being rich or well off

segregation—the act of separating groups, usually based on racial or religious differences

subjugate—enslave or rule a person or group

READ MORE

Alexander, Michelle. *The New Jim Crow: Mass Incarceration in the Age of Colorblindness.* New York: The New Press, 2012.

Hooks, Gwendolyn. *If You Were a Kid During the Civil Rights Movement.* New York: Children's Press/Franklin Watts Trade, 2017.

McWhorter, Diane. *Carry Me Home: Birmingham, Alabama: The Climactic Battle of the Civil Rights Revolution.* New York: Simon and Schuster, 2013.

Williams, Juan. *Eyes on the Prize: America's Civil Rights Years.* New York: Penguin Books, 2013.

CRITICAL THINKING QUESTIONS

1. Do you think the use of "peaceful resistance" was the best way to integrate the South? Why or why not?
2. What role did media attention and publicity play in helping pass civil rights legislation?
3. What do you think might have been the reason for the racism of people in the South? What about the North?